HAPPY OR RIGHT?

BY H. JOI LILIBET

HAPPY OR RIGHT?

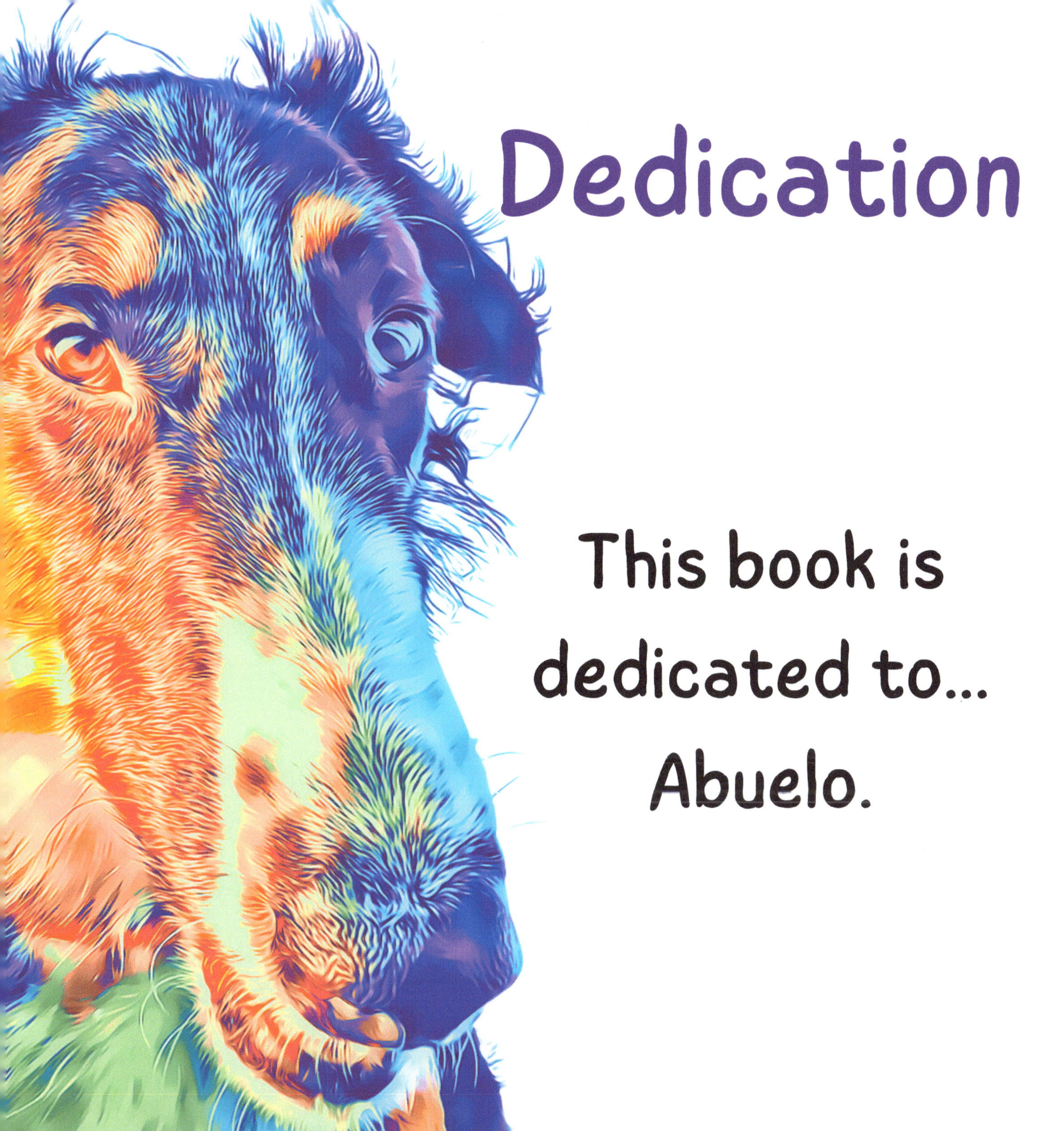

Dedication

This book is
dedicated to...
Abuelo.

Do I want to stop playing to
put you in your place-

Or would I rather just keep this big smile upon my face?

Would I rather keep singing this delicious tune?

Or stop
just to
make
you feel
like a
silly
loon?

One is heart and
the other is
mind –

Both are a part
of me and both
are fine -

But isn't feeling
happy more
easy and fun-

Than
fussing
&
fighting
to make
you feel
wrong?

It's all
available
for me
to do

But what feels better - love,
or the need to prove?

For when I
feel inside
strong and
calm -

I don't try
to make
anyone else
follow along!

When I'm
lit up from
within
I'm bright
as a star -

So everyone else can be exactly where they are!

When I'm rocking comfortable
in my own skin -

Others can show up in whatever shape that they are in!

When
I'm
feeling
my own
shining
light -

It doesn't matter if another is
being dim or bright!

When I'm
feeling the
most sparkly
& glittery -

Right or
wrong simply
never occurs
to me!

And even when I have to
make a choice between
happy and right -

I know deep
down inside
happy will
always give
me flight!

For being happy
gives me my
wings that
lift me up
to be -

The truest
version - of the
most joyful
Razzle-Dazzle ME!!!

www.ingramcontent.com/pod-product-compliance
Lightning Source LLC
Chambersburg PA
CBHW042139030726
47599CB00002B/541